THE MARVEL®

X·MEN®

W9-BLI-421

GUIDE BOOK

BY DWIGHT JON ZIMMERMAN

PARACHUTE
PRESS, INC

Parachute Press, Inc.
156 Fifth Avenue
New York, NY 10010

Published by Parachute Press, Inc.

ISBN: 0-938753-69-X

First printing: September 1992

Printed in the U.S.A.

Design by Bob Feldgus

Contents

TM

Professor X

Introduction

Welcome to the wild world of the most incredible comic book super heroes of all, the X-Men! They have muscles. They have fabulous powers. They fight terrible, evil enemies in battles that span the universe. That's why X-Men comics are *super*-popular! In 1991, a new X-Men title, *X-Men #1,* set a comic book world record by selling 8.2 million (that's 8,200,000) copies!

The X-Men are different from most other Marvel Super Heroes. Other super heroes started out as normal humans, then something strange happened, which left them with extraordinary powers. For example, Peter Parker started out as a normal guy. Then he was bitten by a radioactive spider and became Spider-Man. Bruce Banner was hit by a power-packed gamma ray and turned into the Hulk. Steve Rogers, now known as Captain America, was a scrawny teenager until he volunteered to be injected with a powerful formula by military doctors during World War II.

The X-Men are different from humans, and they never were normal humans. They were born with their super powers. They're mutants. They became mutants because their parents were exposed to powerful radiation before they were born. Some of the X-Men had human parents. Other heroes and heroines in the X-Men teams were born to parents who already were mutants. All the X-Men (and many of them are women!) have dedicated their lives to using their super powers for good, so that one day mutants and humans can live together in peace.

A Mutant with a Dream

The first X-Men team was created by Professor Charles Xavier. To the outside world, Professor Xavier was a respected scientist. People didn't know he was a mutant. Professor X is the most powerful telepath on Earth! He can send messages from his mind to anyone he wants, anywhere in the world. On top of that, he can read other people's minds. Professor X's mutant mind is also a weapon. He can create mental energy bolts that shoot out of his head and can knock out or hypnotize an enemy. Since he respects all life, even that of his enemies, Professor X rarely uses this power.

Professor X could see there was going to be trouble on Earth between normal humans, *Homo sapiens,* and the growing numbers of mutants with super powers, or *Homo sapiens superior.* Because of the mutants' special powers, Professor X knew there was a strong chance that normal people would fear mutants. He decided to pledge his life to the cause of helping mankind and mutantkind live together in peace.

Professor X is always prevented from realizing

Juggernaut

™

this goal by Evil Mutants who want to rule Earth and make humans into slaves.

Another major threat to Professor X's dream is a powerful enemy, Cain Marko, who is also his stepbrother. Cain Marko always was jealous of Charles's powers when they were growing up. Then, when both Charles Xavier and Cain Marko were in the army, Cain Marko stumbled onto incredible powers of his own.

The stepbrothers were stationed in Asia. Cain deserted during an attack by guerrillas. Professor X went after him to bring him back. He followed Cain into a cave that contained an ancient temple. In the temple was a gigantic idol, and in the idol's lap was a large, glowing ruby called the Ruby of Cyttorak. Cain grabbed the jewel. The moment he touched it, a strange glow surrounded him. Cain Marko was transformed into a superstrong giant weighing over 900 pounds. Nothing—not even the impact of an enormous bomb—can hurt him. Cain Marko became an unstoppable human battering ram called Juggernaut, who is one of Professor X's most dangerous enemies!

To fight all evil threats, Professor X formed a group of good mutants who would become the champions of both mankind and other good mutants. This group would stand up against the Evil Mutants and the mutant-hating humans.

The Computer Connection

Professor X designed and programmed a special super computer he called Cerebro to help him form his team of good mutants. Cerebro searches for a special type of mental-energy wave that only mutants' minds make. Only Professor X knows exactly how Cerebro works, and he's not telling anyone.

With Cerebro's help, Professor X located five teenagers with astonishing mutant powers. He opened a school just north of New York City called Professor Xavier's School for Gifted Youngsters. When the students weren't studying math, science, or the humanities, they were exercising their powers—training themselves for combat against Evil Mutants and other enemies! These special teenagers were the first X-Men.

Since that original group, many other mutants have joined the X-Men. New teams of super mutants who believe in Professor X's vision of a peaceful world where mutants and humans can live together were formed. After the original X-Men came a team called the new X-Men. Then two other teams, X-Factor and X-Force, were formed. Next the X-Men split into two teams of their own: the Blue Strike Force and the Gold Strike Force.

The super heroes in each of these groups often switch teams for certain missions or battles, making it hard to keep clear who's on what team at what time. And then to further complicate matters, some of the members of the new X-Men left to join with super mutants in England who had never been a part of any X-team to create an entirely new super hero squad called Excalibur!

Got all that? Don't worry, even the X-Men have a hard time keeping track of everyone. But help is here. The *Marvel X-Men Guide Book* is x-actly what you need to make you an X-Men x-pert.

In this book, you'll find out which X-Men are the strongest and the strangest. You'll read about their early days—and their latest adventures. You'll even get a sneak peak at the top-secret Danger Room. And—watch out—you'll also meet some of the X-Men's fiercest foes and relive their most bruising battles.

The Latest and the Greatest: Today's X-Men

Who are today's X-Men? Where do they live? And—well, one question at a time. Let's start with the basic idea or purpose of today's X-Men. They're an extraordinary lineup composed of original members, veterans with years of combat experience, and new recruits. The list is an honor roll of super heroes: Wolverine, Cyclops, Beast, Storm, Iceman, Jean Grey, Archangel, Colossus, Rogue, Psylocke, Gambit, and Jubilee. And of course there's the man who started it all: Professor X himself, Charles Xavier!

There are actually *two* X-Men teams—the Blue Strike Force and the Gold Strike Force—because there are now so many foes that the X-Men need more mutants and more power to respond to any threat, anywhere. And if the danger demands it, members of one team will temporarily join the other and vice versa. The X-Men's adventures have caused them to travel the world and sometimes into outer space. They've even taken their battles into other dimensions!

The X-Men live on a large estate in Westchester County, just north of New York City. We're talking huge—the land is over three miles long and a mile wide! The estate has a gigantic mansion that has living quarters for more than twelve people plus guests. The mansion has a super-training center called the Danger Room (see Chapter 6), and a hangar and runway for a supersonic jet.

Hidden somewhere in the X-Men Mansion is Cerebro, the X-Men's amazing mutant-detecting computer system. Not only can Cerebro's "mutant radar" find mutants, it can also discover what kinds of superhuman abilities mutants have and how powerful they are. Remember, Cerebro was invented by Professor X in order for him to find and track all mutant activity. He used it to find the mutant teens who became the original X-Men.

Now let's get to the teams themselves. Here's the roll call of today's X-Men, but don't be surprised if it changes soon. If there's one thing that stays the same about the X-Men, it's the fact that their ranks are always changing!

The X-Men Gold Strike Force

Storm—She is the leader of the team. Her real name is Ororo Munroe. To the African tribe who worshipped her, her name meant Beautiful Windrider. Storm can fly by commanding the wind to lift and carry her to incredible heights. She can create life-giving rainfalls or raging thunderstorms.

For years she was happily living in Africa, bringing rain to the tribe's crops and protecting her people from harm. But that life ended when Professor X came to the village and asked her to

Storm

join the X-Men. Though it was a difficult decision, Storm agreed to use her powers to help him.

Colossus—Peter Rasputin is a gentle man, born in the heart of the vast Russian plains called steppes. But when injustice strikes, the gentle giant turns himself into a champion of living steel known as Colossus. As Colossus, almost nothing—not even a bomb blast—can hurt him! His strength is equally incredible. He can shatter granite boulders the size of a house with his fist. In his heart of hearts, he would love to return to his native land and live out his life in peace. But he knows that his mutant gift has given him great responsibilities. Until the battle against the Evil Mutants is finally won, Colossus won't desert his friends, the X-Men.

Jean Grey—Jean Grey's mutant powers can be summed up in the phrase "mind over matter." Jean, who used to be called Marvel Girl, has a power called telekinesis that gives her the ability to lift, move, and handle objects as small as a pin or as large as a truck, using only her mind. Though she can't fly like Storm, she can use her power to carry herself high into the sky.

Her enemies have discovered that it's almost impossible to keep her a prisoner. With her mental power, Jean can untie any rope and unlock any lock! She also creates beams and balls of highly charged energy and can throw them with the speed of thought at any enemy.

Jean Grey

TM

14

Iceman

Iceman—Robert Drake has the coolest power of all—the power to make ice! He can turn himself into a living iceman. He can take water from anywhere—a water faucet, a river or lake, or even the humidity from the air—and make incredibly thick ice walls, ice spears, snowballs, ice cages, ice slides—almost anything he wants. Iceman's the ideal person to have at a party—you'll never run out of ice, not even on the hottest day.

Archangel—His real name is Warren Worthington III, and though he's a multimillionaire who has enjoyed the best that money can buy, he has also suffered great tragedy.

He was born with wings and could fly. As Angel, he was one of the original members of the X-Men. He later left the X-Men and went into semiretirement. Then he joined his old teammates and became a founding member of X-Factor. While on a mission with X-Factor, he was captured by the Evil Mutant Apocalypse, who tore off his wings.

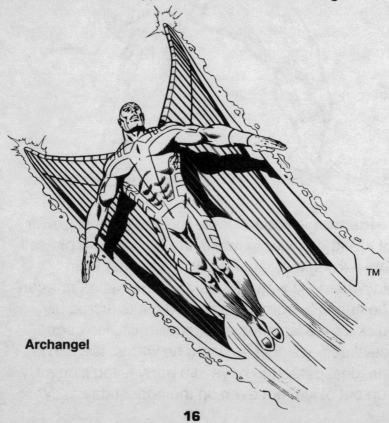

™

Archangel

Then Apocalypse made new wings for him out of a strange biometallic compound. Apocalypse tried to brainwash the wounded and weak Angel and turn him into his servant. He even gave Angel a new name, Archangel. Angel kept the new name, but he did not turn evil. He rebelled against Apocalypse and used the power and weapons of his new wings to defeat him.

Archangel's wings are incredible inventions. With them he can fly faster than the speed of sound! And he can shoot his metallic "feathers" with incredible speed. The "feathers" are razor sharp and coated with a chemical that temporarily paralyzes even the mightiest enemy.

Because of what Apocalypse did to him, Archangel is often silent and moody. But when danger strikes, no one is more dependable in battle than Archangel!

The X-Men Blue Strike Force

Cyclops—The original leader of the X-Men leads the Blue Team into battle. Cyclops, whose real name is Scott Summers, can shoot powerful beams of force he calls optic blasts from his eyes with pinpoint accuracy. These optic beams are so powerful, they can shatter a solid steel door! Unfortunately, they're also uncontrollable. Cyclops has to wear special red goggles all the time.

Cyclops is not the only member of his family

fighting to make the world a better place for mutants and mankind. His younger brother, Havok, helps in the battle, too, as the present-day leader of X-Factor!

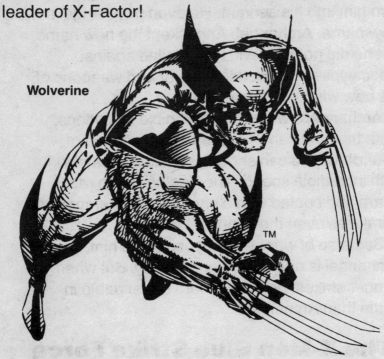

Wolverine

TM

Wolverine—When the going gets really tough, the X-Men call on their greatest fighter, Wolverine. Wolverine calls himself Logan. Nobody's sure if that's his real name, and no one—not even Professor X—has dared to ask!

Much of Wolverine's past is a mystery. All we know for sure is that Wolverine got his Adamantium claws and skeleton in the top-secret Weapon X program, which was engineered by a secret criminal conclave. Adamantium is an ultrastrong, unbreakable metal. As a result his bones are shatterproof, and his claws can slice through the toughest armor like a hot knife through butter. And with his extraordinary animal-like tracking abilities, Wolverine can follow even the faintest trail. The scientists in the Weapon X program planned to turn Wolverine into a living fighting machine and use him for their own evil purposes. Wolverine rebelled and destroyed the whole Weapon X complex.

Wolverine then lived like a savage animal, deep in the woods. While James MacDonald Hudson, an official in a secret department of the Canadian government, and his wife, Heather, were honeymooning in Canada's Wood Buffalo National Park, Wolverine attacked them. Heather shot and wounded Wolverine. Then she and her husband nursed Wolverine back to health and tamed some of the wildness in him.

Wolverine later went to work for the Canadian government, which gave him the code name Weapon X. He was even a member of its super-hero team, Alpha Flight. He left Alpha Flight to join the new X-Men. Wolverine has been with the X-Men ever since.

Wolverine is an expert in hand-to-hand combat—and he has had *many* fights! One reason Wolverine has survived all his battles is his incredible mutant healing factor. In minutes, even the worst of wounds disappears.

Gambit—Anything Gambit touches can become a weapon. With his mutant power he can take the stored, potential energy in any object and turn it into explosive energy. A basketball can become as powerful as a bomb once Gambit touches it.

Though Gambit is with the X-Men, he's not sure how long he wants to stay with the team. Maybe the reason is that he's been a loner for so long—no one even knows his real name—that he has a hard time adjusting to living, working, and fighting with others. Regardless, he plans to remain with them for the near future.

Beast—Hank McCoy, otherwise known as Beast, looks like a big, blue-furred monster. Beast is incredibly strong and amazingly agile. He weighs 350 pounds and can hang upside down by only one foot! Though he looks scary, he's really a nice guy. Not only that, he's a genius! Beast is one of the leading experts in biochemistry. When he's not fighting Evil Mutants or other enemies, he's usually in a laboratory, working on some new experiment that will help mankind.

Hank McCoy was born with the mutant powers of super strength and agility. Originally he looked as normal as any other person, though his hands and feet were a little larger than everyone else's. The blue-furred monster look came as a result of an accident. He drank an experimental formula he had just created. It was definitely not a good thing

Gambit

TM

to do, because the next thing he knew, he had become this big, blue-furred monster!

Beast

™

Rogue—She can fly fast as lightning, and not only do bullets and cannon shells bounce off her super-tough skin, she also has the mutant ability to steal the powers of anyone she touches! That's right, all she has to do is touch someone with her hand, or any part of her body, and she will instantly have that person's power. So if she grabs Cyclops, she'll be able to shoot optic eye beams. If she touches Wolverine, she'll get claws, etc. That's the neat part of her power. The bad part is that she can't control her power-stealing ability. To protect herself and her friends from the consequences of accidental contact, she wears a bodysuit all the time.

Rogue

TM

Psylocke—An unbeatable expert in martial arts and telepathy, Elisabeth Braddock is almost as dangerous as Wolverine when it comes to close-in fighting. What makes Psylocke unbeatable in battle is her "psychic blade." It's an energy sword she creates with her mind. Anyone touched by this "psychic blade" is instantly knocked out.

Being a super hero is a family tradition for Psylocke: her brother is Captain Britain, leader of Excalibur, the good mutant team based in England. (For more on them, turn to Chapter 3.)

Psylocke

™

24

Jubilee—Jubilation Lee is the youngest member of the X-Men team. Professor X refuses to let her take part in battles because she's a teenager. Somehow she still manages to get into the thick of the fighting. And the X-Men are usually glad that she does. Jubilee can create balls of energy that explode with dazzling results. These "flash/bang" effects are more than just show—they can totally disorient an enemy.

Jubilee can't wait to grow up. Because when she does, her dream of becoming a full-fledged X-Men member will become a reality!

TM

Jubilee

The X-citing History of the X-Men

Today's X-Men are just the tip of the iceberg when it comes to knowing the full X-Men story. To get the whole story, we have to go back to the time when Professor Charles Xavier brought five teenage mutants to his School for Gifted Youngsters.

Professor X's first students were Scott Summers, Jean Grey, Hank McCoy, Robert Drake, and Warren Worthington III. Professor X gave them code names in order to protect their real identities. Scott became Cyclops, Jean was Marvel Girl, Hank became Beast, Robert Drake became Iceman, and Warren Worthington III was Angel. The code names quickly became a part of each member's identity. Teammates often call each other by the code name rather than by the person's real name.

School Days

When they started out, the original five were not the well-trained fighting force they are today. Though they had extraordinary powers that made them different, in every other respect they were normal, healthy teenagers. They had the same hopes, dreams, problems, and fears that all teens have.

They loved movies, television, skipping homework, going out, and teasing each other. Of course, their teasing had some pretty wild twists to it. Iceman turned out to be the biggest practical joker. He loved doing things such as putting ice in Beast's shoes, or coating bedsheets with ice, or having snowball fights in the middle of a July heat wave!

Under Professor X's guidance, the teens grew to accept themselves and their awesome powers. While still in their teens, the young X-Men fought the first of many battles against Magneto, the Evil Mutant. Magneto was then and still is one of the X-Men's most feared foes (see Chapter 4).

Magneto has the ability to control the power of magnetism. With a wave of his hand, Magneto can cause a car or a tank to fly into the air, and with another wave of his hand, he can shatter it. While in their teens, the X-Men fought other foes, too, including the mysterious Vanisher, the immovable Blob, Unus the Untouchable, and Professor X's stepbrother, the unstoppable Juggernaut.

But the X-Men didn't fight all the time. Even though they were mutants battling to save the world, they did try to live as close to a normal life as possible. Hank (Beast) and Robert (Iceman) were two guys who just wanted to have fun. On the weekends, when there was no schoolwork—or Evil Mutant fighting—they somehow always managed to find dates. Warren Worthington III (Angel), would even strap down his wings and hide them under a customized suit in order to find a date. Girls almost fainted when they saw this handsome guy with the broadest shoulders ever!

X-Men in Love

But the real romance was the one between Scott Summers (Cyclops) and Jean Grey (Marvel Girl). Unfortunately, even though the two loved each other, they didn't tell each other! You see, Scott always was the strong, silent type who took his role as leader of the X-Men ultraseriously. He was worried that he couldn't be a good leader if he told Jean how he felt about her. He was also afraid she might reject him.

Jean loved Scott just as much as he loved her, but she was intimidated by his coldness. She couldn't tell if he loved her or hated her. She was afraid to tell him her feelings because she was afraid of being rejected, too.

And to top it all off, Professor X and the X-Men could see that the two heroes were hopelessly in love! They finally managed to tell each other how they felt, in spite of their fears. That was quite a while ago. Some pretty weird things have happened to the relationship since then, but through thick and thin, they continue to love each other and keep their relationship going strong.

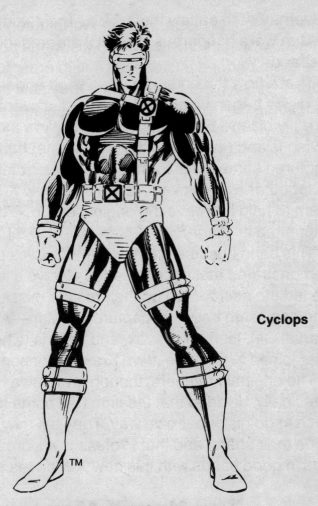

Cyclops

™

Hard to Be Heroes

In the beginning, humans were glad the X-Men were around, and they liked and admired them. Unfortunately, that changed. Anti-mutant feelings began to spread. Still, the X-Men battled on, holding true to Professor X's dream. Eventually, though, powerful groups convinced the U.S.

government to outlaw the X-Men. They said the X-Men were dangerous. The FBI ordered them to disband.

That's how the original X-Men saga ended. The next part began when Professor X discovered that a really bizarre Evil Mutant called Krakoa the Living Island (and it was the size of one) had captured some of his former students. Professor X, together with Cyclops, recruited a *new* X-Men team to help him save the original group. (This happened in *Giant-Size X-Men #1*—1975.)

This band became the new X-Men. Cyclops demonstrated that once a leader, always a leader. He led the new X-Men on their rescue mission. The new team freed the captured X-Men—Angel, Marvel Girl, Iceman, Havok, and Polaris (who later joined X-Factor)—from Krakoa's prison.

The original members, though grateful to be free finally, decided that the time had come for each to go his or her own way. They felt they had done their share, and that Professor X's dream was in good hands with this new X-Men team.

The New X-Men

Thus the stage was set for the adventures of what's considered the greatest team in the X-Men's history. Though others came and went during the initial period, the core of the new X-Men was Cyclops, Wolverine, Storm, Colossus, Nightcrawler, and Marvel Girl (yes, there were some mutants who were a part of the original team that stayed on!). Kitty Pryde joined up and took the code name Shadowcat. (Nightcrawler and Shadowcat later joined Excalibur—for more on them, turn to Chapter 3.)

These new X-Men were all older than the original group Professor X first brought together. They didn't need the schooling and guidance Professor X gave to the original teens. While holding true to Professor X's dream, they could act more independently. This allowed Professor X to devote some time to a new generation of students he had found with the help of Cerebro and brought to his school. He called this group the New Mutants.

Meanwhile, the new X-Men's first challenge turned out to be getting along with each other! Cyclops and the fierce Wolverine were always at each other's throats. Everyone else was usually caught somewhere in the middle of these confrontations. Only time and the kind of friendship that comes from being together in life-and-death battles solved that problem.

Good-bye, Professor X

And what battles they had! They dealt with the world-destroying powers and fought in outer space against a bizarre menace called the Brood. During this battle, Professor X decided to leave the X-Men and stay with the woman he loved,

Empress Lilandra. Empress Lilandra rules an alien race called Shi'ar. The Shi'ar galactic empire is one of the mightiest the universe has ever known.

The parting between the X-Men and Professor X was tough. The X-Men were happy that Professor X had found someone to love, but they were upset that he'd be living on the other side of the galaxy! Eventually, they said good-bye, and the new X-Men returned to Earth to continue his cause.

But when the X-Men returned, they discovered that antimutant and Evil Mutant activity was stronger than ever—and growing!

Calling All X-Men!

The X-Men fought in a war called Inferno, where demons from another dimension tried to take over Earth. They fought in a worldwide antimutant conflict started by a high-tech mutant-hating organization called the Right. Mutants who had at one time or another been X-Men returned to the X-Men Mansion and rejoined the fight to help stop the growing antimutant threat.

They formed the two X-Men teams—the Blue Strike Force and the Gold Strike Force—in *X-Men #1*—1991. Though each group has different members, both are dedicated to the same purpose—working to help mankind and mutantkind live together in peace.

X-tra Teams

Over the years X-Men members have broken off into other mutant super-hero teams. Here's a rundown on what they are, and who fights in each one.

Excalibur

They're based in England and have as their headquarters a custom-built lighthouse that sits on a gateway that opens to other dimensions! Captain Britain and his team, Excalibur, were brought together by an attack on England by Warwolves, bizarre body-snatchers from another dimension. After Excalibur defeated the Warwolves, they decided that since they had worked so well as a team, they should remain one.

They called themselves Excalibur, after legendary King Arthur's great sword. Unlike the other teams who fight Evil Mutants or mutant-haters on Earth, Excalibur battles enemies that come from other dimensions! Sometimes they even chase the enemies back into their own dimension.

Here are some of the super heroes who make up Excalibur:

Captain Britain—Brian Braddock is the real name of Captain Britain, the leader of Excalibur.

He's big, he's strong, and he can fly superfast. And, according to some mutants, he's one of the most stubborn and impulsive mutants on the planet! His sister is Psylocke, the X-Men's psychic martial arts expert.

Captain Britain

TM

Nightcrawler—Kurt Wagner is another Excalibur member who started out in the X-Men. He looks like a demon, but in fact, he's one of the most happy-go-lucky people you'll ever meet! Nightcrawler's an incredible acrobat. He's also a great swordsman. He can fight with three swords, one in each hand and one in his highly flexible tail! Nightcrawler also has the mutant ability to teleport—that is, travel instantly—from one place to another. With a quick mental command, he can disappear and reappear anywhere he wants in the immediate area. There's just one problem, though: the smell caused by the teleportation is disgusting! Compared to it, rotten eggs smell like perfume!

Nightcrawler

TM

Shadowcat

TM

Shadowcat— Once a member of the new X-Men, Shadowcat's real name is Kitty Pryde. Her mutant power is called "phasing." That means she can walk through walls, or anything else for that matter—even people! You could say that enemies don't stand a "ghost" of a chance keeping her a prisoner.

X-Factor

X-Factor is unique among all the mutant super-hero groups—it's an organization of the federal government! X-Factor's orders are to investigate the odd, the bizarre, and the unlikely—in other words, anything that's too strange for the FBI or the CIA to handle. Their official government liaison is Special Agent Valerie Cooper, who goes with them on every mission (of course, since she doesn't have mutant powers, she can only watch, not help). X-Factor hopes that through their highly publicized actions, they can prove to mankind that mutants can contribute to society. Here are some mutants who make up the team:

Havok—Alex Summers, leader of X-Factor, is the younger brother of Scott Summers, also known as Cyclops. Havok has the ability to absorb ultrapowerful cosmic energy and throw it at any object in his path. When Havok powers up, his enemies usually run away as fast as they can! Havok started out with the X-Men. Then he left to go on his own. Now he works with his brother Cyclops whenever The Blue Strike Force teams up with X-Factor.

Polaris—Lorna Dane was once a member of the X-Men, too. Like Magneto, she possesses the mutant power of magnetism. She can lift metal objects of almost any size, create super-tough energy shields that are virtually unbreakable, and

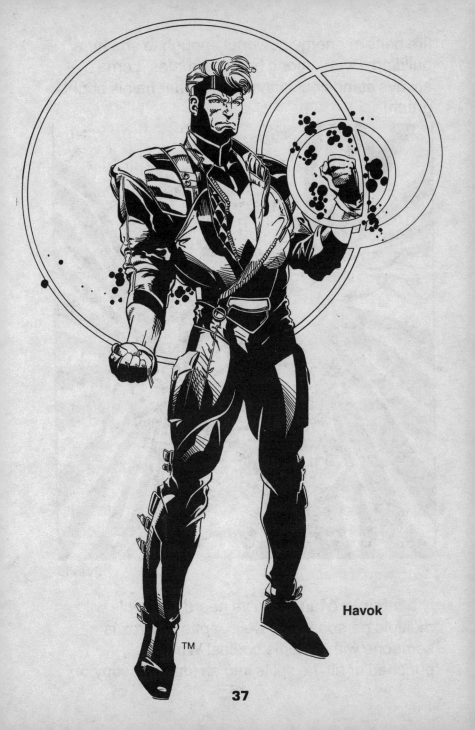

Havok

™

fire bolts of energy powerful enough to shatter a building. Even among her teammates, Lorna always stands out in the crowd—her hair is bright green!

Polaris

Multiple Man—You've heard of people with multiple personalities; well, Jamie Madrox is someone with multiple bodies! When he's punched or hit, he splits into an identical copy of

Multiple Man

TM

Quicksilver

™

himself. The more times he's hit, the more copies of himself he makes. Even though he's not super-strong, he can overwhelm an enemy by creating an instant army! To help control his power, he wears a special bodysuit that's supposed to absorb the impact of normal blows. Unfortunately, in the kinds of places Jamie goes, there's no such thing as a "normal" blow.

Quicksilver—Pietro Maximoff has the mutant power of super speed. Some mutants also think that he's got the super power of being able instantly to rub people the wrong way. He was originally an enemy of the X-Men, but he rejected the Evil Mutants' plan to enslave all humans and rule the world. With the anti-mutant movement gaining strength, he decided the X-Men's cause needed the services of the world's greatest super hero, himself. Now he's with X-Factor, and they're happy that he is!

X-Force

X-Force began as the group called the New Mutants. They were the second team of teenage mutants brought together by Professor X at his special school near the X-Men Mansion. Just as he did with the first X-Men team, Professor X combined regular school classes and special training to teach the super teens how to use their powers. Of all the X-Men spin-off teams, X-Force is the youngest. But any enemy who thinks they're pushovers because they're young quickly finds out how wrong he or she is! The New Mutants changed their name to X-Force because they're no longer students, and they've grown into a tough, full-fledged, fighting team.

Here are some members of the team:

Cable—He's a cyborg (half-man, half-machine) and the leader of X-Force. He's one tough fighter, as his enemies well know. In addition to being an expert with almost every weapon ever created, Cable also has telekinetic powers just like Marvel Girl. Not only that, but he's got a weird, glowing bionic eye that lets him see things even in the darkest night, and an even stranger biomechanical arm that's incredibly strong! No one knows much about his past except that he's been fighting in wars all his life. His philosophy is that only the strongest and toughest will survive. And he's vowed to make the X-Force team the strongest and toughest of all the mutant super hero teams. Since Cable has been a soldier and a fighter all his life, the X-Force team is trained in combat exercises that would exhaust most members of the X-Men.

Cannonball—Sam Guthrie's code name says it all. When he flies through the air, he's like an unbreakable living cannonball that can smash its way through almost anything! For someone with so much power, he's pretty shy. Quite a few girls, including his X-Force teammate, Boom Boom,

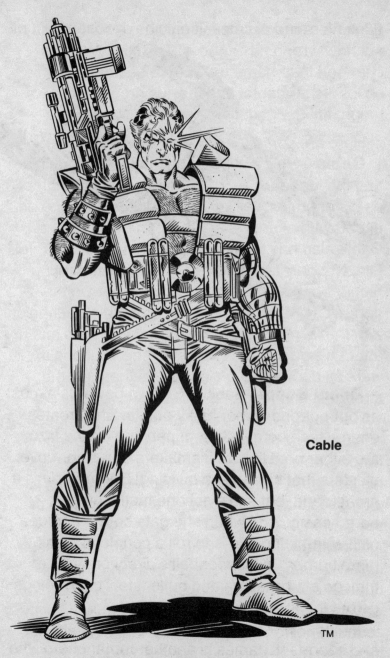

Cable

TM

43

think he's kind of cute—if only he'd loosen up a bit.

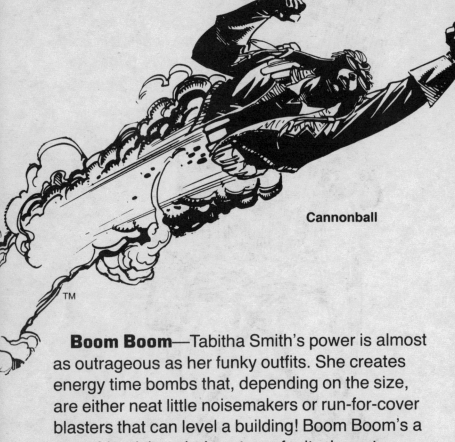

Cannonball

™

Boom Boom—Tabitha Smith's power is almost as outrageous as her funky outfits. She creates energy time bombs that, depending on the size, are either neat little noisemakers or run-for-cover blasters that can level a building! Boom Boom's a great friend, but she's got one fault: she gets bored easily. And when she gets bored, her idea of livening things up is to roll a couple of small "time bombs" in Cannonball's direction. When they go off, boredom and quite a few other things go out the window!

Warpath—James Proudstar is superstrong and superfast. James is another mutant hero who had a family member in the X-Men ranks. His brother, John—code named Thunderbird—was a member of the new X-Men. John died in one of the new X-Men's first missions. James has vowed that his brother's sacrifice will not have been in vain.

Warpath

Shatterstar—He's a hero who's literally out of this world! Shatterstar's the ultimate warrior from another dimension in the future. Shatterstar's

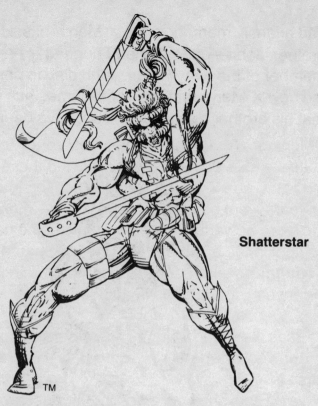

Shatterstar

™

fighting ability is unmatched. He knows every martial arts skill that exists, his reflexes are faster than lightning, and he has an ability to learn instantly how to master any weapon. His purpose was to help overthrow the tyrants ruling his world. But he was chased from his world and his dimension by the tyrants' troops. Now he's on Earth, proving to be the best fighter on the X-Force team, better even than Cable!

X-Men Hall of Shame

Talk about your slimeballs. For every great X-Men hero, there's a terrible villain ready to make life miserable for everyone. And these guys don't quit. The X-Men have been fighting Magneto for years—but he always comes back—meaner and more powerful than before. In fact, he has the top spot in the all-time X-Men Hall of Shame.

Magneto—He's the most dangerous Evil Mutant on Earth. But as famous (or infamous) as he is, there is still a lot about him that's a mystery. He uses the name Magnus from time to time, but no one knows where he was born, or what his real name is.

We do know he was a prisoner in Auschwitz, a World War II Nazi concentration camp. During this time he actually did have superhuman powers, but he either didn't realize it, or he was unable to use them because he was so weak.

Magneto was the only one in his family to survive the concentration camps. After he was freed, he married and had children. But when his wife discovered he had extraordinary abilities, she became deathly afraid of him, took the children, and left him.

At first Magneto used his power for the cause of good. He went to Israel and met Professor X. This

Magneto

™

was before Professor X had formed the X-Men. Magneto helped Professor X defeat the high-tech terrorist organization called HYDRA. After that, the two men went their separate ways.

Magneto's control over the power of magnetism became almost limitless. He could lift a 30,000-ton object (that's 60,000,000 pounds!) into the air just by concentrating his will. With his mental energy he could assemble machinery. He could also shoot all kinds of energy, heat, light, or radio waves, from his head or his hands!

While he was learning how to use his power, Magneto made a fateful decision. He decided that the only way to be sure mutants were safe from humans was for the mutants to conquer humans. Magneto began his crusade to rule the world and make himself emperor of Earth!

Magneto made his first bid for power by seizing the American missile base Cape Citadel. This act of war prompted Professor X to send the original X-Men into their first battle. Magneto demanded that all mankind surrender to him. If mankind refused to acknowledge Magneto as their master, he would start World War III!

It took a lot of courage, fighting—and a mutant-sized dose of good luck—for the X-Men to stop Magneto's mad plan, but stop him they did. Unfortunately, Magneto escaped capture and vowed vengeance on the X-Men. Each time he makes a grab for world power, the X-Men find a way to stop him. Even after Magneto created the superpowerful group called the Brotherhood of Evil Mutants to fight the X-Men, the heroes still managed to defeat him.

Magneto's attempts to dominate the world continued for years. Finally he made an all-out bid for power. Once again the X-Men rose up to challenge and stop him. During the incredible battle that resulted, Magneto severely injured the teenager Shadowcat. He instantly regretted his actions and, for the first time, began to question the violent path he had chosen. Soon Magneto announced that he had changed his ways. The reason was true love.

A non-mutant woman named Aleytys Forrester had saved Magneto from being killed by a strange alien being called the Beyonder. Magneto and Aleytys fell in love. Something later happened to this relationship, and they broke up. No one has seen Aleytys for years. Magneto refuses to talk about what happened between them, probably because it would bring back so much pain.

Obviously his great love for Aleytys helped change Magneto's attitude about humans. He decided that his war against mankind was wrong, and that he would now try to help humans and the X-Men. Magneto became temporary leader of the New Mutants (the X-Force team before they took the name X-Force) in Professor X's absence. And for a while, he actually did try to be a super hero.

Unfortunately, his attempt to be a mutant super hero had failed. He left the X-Men. No one, not the X-Men nor the humans, would trust him. Wherever Magneto went, he was attacked. Magneto decided he wanted to be left totally alone.

He rejected all contact with everyone, mutants and humans. But recently, in *X-Men #1*—1991, Magneto decided that it truly was impossible for humans and mutants to live together in peace as long as humans ruled Earth. At the desperate request of a group of Evil Mutants who were being hunted by a renegade troop of high-tech human soldiers, Magneto once again became the leader of the Evil Mutants.

Apocalypse—Apocalypse, who can change his size to make himself either tiny or huge, shares Magneto's dream of Evil Mutant rule. The difference is that Apocalypse sees himself as the #1 Evil Mutant! Apocalypse believes that there will be an all-out war between mankind and mutants. Apocalypse has a very brutal method for preparing for that war. He forces other mutants to fight each other, then he takes the winners of these battles and adds to their powers. His goal is to create an unstoppable Evil Mutant army mindlessly loyal to him. It's a goal that will take a long time to reach. But Apocalypse doesn't care. Unlike the other mutants, he's already over a thousand years old!

Apocalypse

Sabretooth—Victor Creed is Wolverine's greatest enemy. In fact, he's the only enemy who's ever beaten Wolverine—not once, but every time they've met! Like Wolverine, he was a part of the mysterious Weapon X program. Sabretooth and Wolverine have the same powers and the same mutant healing ability. But

Sabretooth

TM

Sabretooth is far more savage. Wolverine hunts and kills only when necessary. Sabretooth kills *everything* he hunts, from the smallest animal to any human unfortunate enough to cross his path.

Juggernaut

Juggernaut—Cain Marko sees his fight against the X-Men and their allies as a personal one, because he's the stepbrother of Professor X. Cain has always been a bully and a troublemaker. Juggernaut's purpose in life is to destroy his stepbrother's vision of a world at peace.

Upstarts—This is the newest group of Evil Mutants, and some members of the X-Men think they're the most dangerous. Their leader is the cunning and cruel Trevor Fitzroy. Their purpose is sport! These callous mutants are in a cruel competition to see who can destroy the most mutants! So any mutant, evil or good, is fair game.

Sauron—Karl Lykos is a mutant who's a life-energy parasite. He eats by draining the

Sauron

TM

energy from living beings. When he drains enough energy, he transforms into the hideous, flying pterodactyl-like Sauron! As Sauron, he has irresistible hypnotic powers that can make anyone his slave.

Sentinels—Sentinels are robots created by Professor Bolivar Trask, a brilliant but misguided

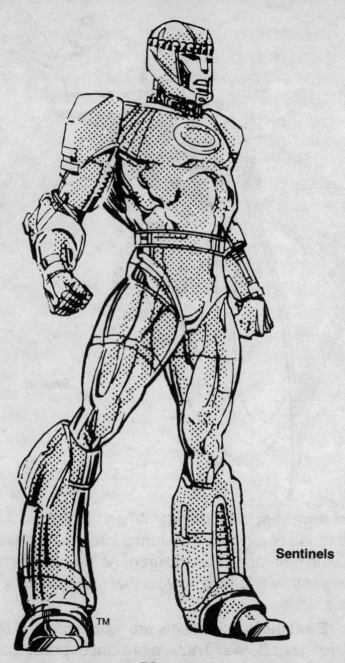

Sentinels

TM

scientist. He created this mechanical army to defend mankind from the threat of mutants. Unfortunately, he made a terrible mistake in the Sentinels' programming. As a result, the Sentinels' computer logic determined that the best way they could protect mankind from mutants was by *ruling* mankind! Dr. Trask died trying to correct his mistake. But the damage had been done. The antimutant hysteria created by Dr. Trask's highly publicized attacks on all mutants caused people and governments to hate not only Evil Mutants, but also X-Men.

After a series of battles, the X-Men thought they defeated and destroyed the Sentinels. But the Sentinels found a way to rebuild themselves. Each new version of the Sentinels was bigger and stronger than the earlier one—they're now up to Model VI. There's even a three-headed Sentinel called the Tri-Sentinel! The X-Men keep battling the Sentinels, but each time gets tougher and tougher for the X-Men to win.

X-Men's Greatest Battles

The X-Men have had some spectacular battles in their long career. More than a few of them were out of this world—and out of this dimension!

The longest and most bitter war the X-Men have fought has been against Magneto. It began when Magneto announced his plan for world conquest by seizing control of a U.S. missile base, and that war continues to this very day. It won't end until either the X-Men or Magneto are totally defeated. Don't hold your breath waiting for that day.

There are lots of other memorable battles in the X-Men's history. Here are some of the more famous ones:

The Dark Phoenix Saga

Phoenix was a member of the new X-Men. Everyone thought she was Jean Grey (Marvel Girl), who had somehow gained more power. It was discovered later that Phoenix was actually an incredibly powerful alien creature who had captured Jean Grey, imprisoned her in a capsule, and buried the capsule under the sea. Jean was kept in suspended animation for years.

Mastermind, an Evil Mutant, wanted to turn Phoenix into a traitor so that she would destroy the X-Men. His plan was to use his hypnotic ability to take control of her mind and force Phoenix to become evil. At first, it seemed that Mastermind's plan had backfired. But gradually Phoenix became more and more evil and uncontrollable.

Whenever Phoenix turned into her evil self, she took the name Dark Phoenix. As Dark Phoenix, she went on a wild spree of destruction. She rocketed into outer space and, in a spectacular display of evil force, destroyed an entire solar system.

Of course, an action like this is going to attract the attention of the authorities. In this case, the authorities were the space-spanning guardians of the most advanced empire in the universe, a people who called themselves the Shi'ar. A whole Shi'ar space fleet was ordered to follow Dark Phoenix and destroy her before she could destroy another solar system. They tracked Dark Phoenix back to Earth and demanded that the X-Men turn her over to them.

The X-Men refused. In an effort to save Phoenix, who had temporarily regained control of her evil side, the X-Men agreed to a gladiator-style battle on Earth's moon against the Shi'ar's greatest warriors. If the X-Men won, then Phoenix would be allowed to live.

But while the battle was going on, Phoenix

Dark Phoenix

TM

realized how dangerous she had become. Just when it seemed that the X-Men were winning the gladiator battle, Phoenix deliberately sacrificed herself in order to stop further harm from coming to anyone, especially the X-Men, whom she had come to love. Jean Grey (Marvel Girl) reappeared

—with absolutely no knowledge of Phoenix or Dark Phoenix. The shock to everyone—especially to her true love, Cyclops—was huge!

X-Men Versus The Avengers

Here's a twist! The X-Men actually defended Magneto against one of the greatest super hero teams of all time, the Avengers! It started when the Avengers announced they were going to capture Magneto and bring him before a world court to be tried for his crimes against humanity. The problem for the X-Men was that the Avengers' decision came at the height of worldwide anti-mutant hysteria. The X-Men believed there was no way that Magneto would get a fair trial. The X-Men fought to keep Magneto away from the Avengers. Magneto later surprised everyone by voluntarily agreeing to go before the court. Ultimately Magneto was allowed to go free, but that verdict only added to mankind's growing hatred of mutants.

Wolverine Versus Sabretooth

This is another ongoing war, and it's one of the most brutal. The hatred between Wolverine and Sabretooth started the very first time they met, before Wolverine got his claws.

It happened in a remote town in the Rocky Mountains. Sabretooth had killed the woman Wolverine loved, and dared Wolverine to try to get him. Sabretooth thought Wolverine would back down—every human who ever faced him did. Wolverine surprised Sabretooth. He attacked. The battle quickly took both fighters deep into the woods. The longer they fought, the more Sabretooth loved it.

The end of this first battle came when both Wolverine and Sabretooth fell off a high cliff. Both of them had mutant healing ability, so they survived. Sabretooth recovered first and, thinking Wolverine was going to die because he didn't know about his mutant powers, left him. When Wolverine awoke, he vowed that he would never rest until he had taken vengeance on Sabretooth.

X-Factor Versus Apocalypse

While X-Factor works to create peace between mankind and the mutants, Apocalypse works to prepare mutants for the eventual all-out war that he believes will come between mutants and mankind. Of course, Apocalypse's plan is to make himself the tyrant leader of Earth when the fighting's done. He's tried to get X-Factor to believe in his cause, and he almost succeeded. But X-Factor managed to discover the truth about Apocalypse's evil scheme. They defeated him and took away the amazing spaceship that was his base of operations.

X-Traordinary Stuff

Being a member of an X-Men team is pretty tough. They've always got bad guys after them. And it's not easy being a mutant to start with! But there are some pluses to the job—the X-Men have some really neat stuff!

The Danger Room

Immediately after Professor X formed the X-Men team, he created a special combat exercise chamber for them. He called this place the Danger Room. And he wasn't fooling! This place was chock-full of every type of threat he could imagine. He knew that since the X-Men had to fight super-powered enemies, they needed a special place that challenged their powers. He also knew the X-Men would be in life-and-death situations, so he made the Danger Room's battle programs as close to real combat conditions as possible.

Fortunately, fail-safe devices were built into the room so that as dangerous as the workouts were, they weren't fatal. Even so, there have been many times when individual X-Men members were seriously injured during a "workout."

CUTAWAY VIEW OF SECOND SUB-BASEMENT
This level of the X-Men Mansion is used for mission planning and training.

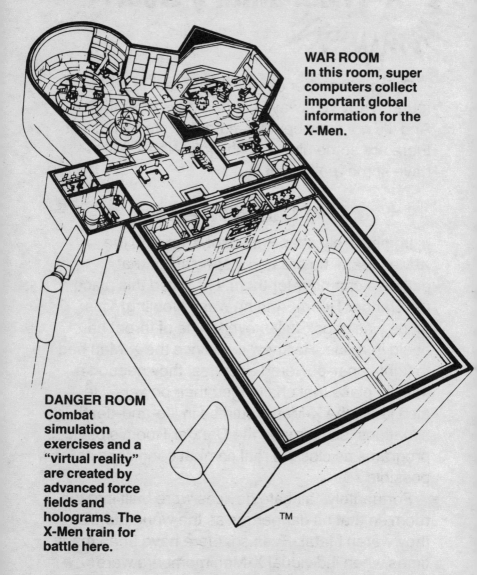

WAR ROOM
In this room, super computers collect important global information for the X-Men.

DANGER ROOM
Combat simulation exercises and a "virtual reality" are created by advanced force fields and holograms. The X-Men train for battle here.

TM

Over the years, the Danger Room has been rebuilt many times. The latest and most extensive remodeling was done with the help of the engineers from the Shi'ar galaxy. It was more or less in repayment for help the X-Men had given them in one of their intergalactic battles.

The Danger Room is located at Sub-Basement Level Two of the X-Men Mansion. It's huge, and thanks to the Shi'ar technology, it can seem as big as all outdoors. Instead of just mechanical devices, the combat simulation exercises are now done with a combination of advanced robots and ultrasophisticated holograms. The computer system can create what computer engineers call "virtual reality," which means that even though the scene isn't real, it's so well created that it seems real. Any type of environment or combat condition can be replicated, from tropical rain forests to outer space, from robot warriors to replicas of Magneto and other enemies. The Danger Room can also be programmed for individual combat if just one X-Men member wants to train, or for group battle for a full-team practice.

Wolverine practices his hunting and tracking ability. This can get wild because the Danger Room can totally recreate sounds and smells of the outdoors!

Nightcrawler, with his acrobatic ability, works out in a really wild "jungle gym" of monkey bars, rings, rods, hooks, handles, and fences.

Archangel usually practices maneuverability in flight. He'll fly through an obstacle course of objects randomly placed in the air or extending from the ceiling. Then there's an even more dangerous practice session in which he is shot by high-powered energy weapons. If Archangel gets hit by one of the energy beams, he'll be paralyzed for a whole day!

Cyclops's sessions usually involve using his powerful optic eye beams. He practices wide-angle high-powered blasts that will destroy three or more Danger Room attack robots, and very thin beams of light that have to go through a keyhole without touching the sides in order to properly unlock a lock.

The X-Men Jet

With all the worldwide troubles going on, the X-Men have to get to antimutant hot-spots ultrafast. Thanks to their specially modified Lockheed RS-150 Blackbird, they can.

From the outside, the X-Men jet looks like the famous Lockheed SR-71 spyplane. But that's where the resemblance ends. Again, thanks to their friends the Shi'ar, the interior and engines have been completely redesigned and made faster, lighter, and tougher. For instance, the Blackbird's maximum speed is now 3,234 miles per hour—over four times the speed of sound. That means that the X-Men's jet can go from New

York City to Los Angeles in about one hour! Of course, all the time they saved getting to the airfield is then lost when they get caught in a traffic jam! Speed isn't the only amazing thing about the Blackbird. It can fly through outer space and has ultrasophisticated Stealth technology that can make it totally invisible to radar and other detection devices.

Cerebro

In addition to finding and gathering information about mutants worldwide, Cerebro is also hooked up to all the defense and electrical systems of the X-Men Mansion and estate. From inside Cerebro's control room, a person can watch everything that happens in the estate and activate a defense system designed to stop the most powerful enemy!

Professor X also invented portable Cerebro units for the X-Men to carry on missions. Wolverine makes a point of not using his—he trusts his abilities more than he trusts any machine, even one made by Professor X!

The Name Game

What's in a name? Well, when it comes to code names for the X-Men, quite a bit! Most of the members, such as Cyclops, had just one . . . well, that's not quite right—Cyclops had another name for a while, Eric the Red. Well, Wolverine just had one name . . . actually, Wolverine had another name, too, Patch. And knowing Wolverine, he might have had others that he's not talking about. All right, Professor X had just one code name, and that's "Professor X"—except when Wolverine called him "Charlie," but out of respect for Professor X, we won't count that.

Different names and nicknames go hand in hand with being a member of the X-Men. Some of them are a lot of fun!

Cyclops: Cyke, Slim, Eric the Red, Boss-Man
Shadowcat: Ariel, Sprite, Kitty, Katya
Storm: Beautiful Windrider, 'Roro
Nightcrawler: Fuzzy Elf
Beast: Hank, Furry, Fuzzball
Wolverine: Patch, Logan, Wolvie
Professor X: Xavier, Charlie (only Wolverine dared use this one)
Colossus: Piotr Nikolievitch
Jean Grey: Marvel Girl, Red

Ask Cerebro

Okay, here's your chance to catch up on some fantastic facts about the X-Men. *The Marvel X-Men Guide Book* is going right to the source—to Cerebro. Cerebro has every amazing fact about the X-Men stored in its megabyte computer brain. Want to know them? Just ask Cerebro.

What is Magneto's real name?

The answer is unknown. There is little data on his early life. Magneto chose the name Magnus for himself, but no one thinks it is his real name. There is no data to reveal why he chose this name.

How much does a Sentinel weigh?

A Sentinel weighs 30 tons, or 60,000 pounds. Do not let it step on you.

How many claws does Wolverine have?

Wolverine has six retractable claws. There are three on each hand. The claws come out of the top of his hand.

Who is the shortest member of the X-Men teams?

This may surprise you. It's Wolverine. He is only 5 feet, 3 inches tall. Jubilee is 5 feet tall, but she is not yet a full member of the X-Men.

How many bathrooms does the X-Men Mansion have?

There are nine bathrooms in the living quarters section of the mansion. Additional bathrooms exist in other sections. But all information about them is classified.

We've seen a number of the X-Men with brothers or sisters on the teams. Does anyone have a parent who's a super hero?

Yes. The father of Cyclops and Havok, Christopher Summers, has the code name Corsair. He is the leader of a group of intergalactic pirates called Starjammers.

Some people think that Sabretooth is the father of Wolverine. But no evidence has been produced that confirms this.

Does Storm have a weakness?

Yes. Storm suffers from severe claustrophobia, which means she's afraid of being in small, closed-in places. This is a result of an accident when she was a child in which a building collapsed on her, and she was buried alive.

How old is Wolverine?

Wolverine is over eighty years old.

If Wolverine is such a great fighter, why isn't he a leader of the X-Men?

Wolverine does not choose to be a leader. He prefers to remain a fighter.

What did Nightcrawler do before he joined the X-Men?

Nightcrawler was an acrobat in a circus in Bavaria, Germany.

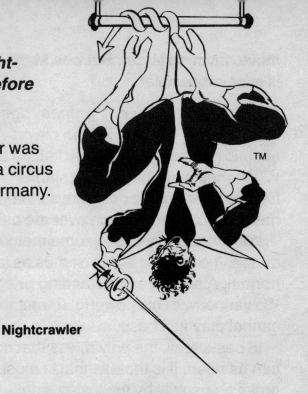

Nightcrawler

How cold can Iceman make himself?

Iceman can drop his temperature to -105.7 degrees Farenheit.

How does Multiple Man get rid of the duplicates of himself?

He can cause them to be reabsorbed into the original body with a conscious and deliberate thought command.

Could Magneto cause Earth to be moved off its orbit if he wanted?

Magneto is very powerful. With his magnetic powers he can move objects as large as a super tanker. He has not demonstrated an ability to move anything larger. But with Magneto, nothing is ever impossible!

Do the X-Men play any games together?

When they can, the X-Men play a variety of athletic games, including basketball and softball. When they play, they try to establish rules that forbid the use of their powers so that no one side has too big an advantage over the other.

With softball, because some members are so strong, the outfield is three times as large as normal. Also, there is a standing rule that Wolverine, with his powerful retractable claws, cannot play first base.

In basketball, the only rule is that no powers can be used. It is the rule that is most often broken—usually by the losing side.

Who exactly are the Shi'ar?

They are an alien race from a distant galaxy. They possess highly advanced technology. Their spaceships can travel faster than the speed of light. Under their leader, the Empress Lilandra, they rule the greatest empire in the galaxy. Empress Lilandra fell in love with Professor X, and for a long time Professor X stayed with her in the Shi'ar empire.

What is Shadowcat's favorite food?

Chocolate ice cream, in a very large container.

Are You an X-Men X-pert?

Now that you've found out about the X-Men and their friends and enemies, we think you've got what it takes to be an X-pert! Just answer the questions below. And if you get five or more right, you can consider yourself a genuine official X-pert!

1) Who was the first X-Men member?
   A) Cyclops
   B) Marvel Girl
   C) Professor X
   D) Lockheed

2) Who was the X-Men's first enemy?
   A) Vanisher
   B) Magneto
   C) Brotherhood of Evil Mutants
   D) The U.S. government

3) Wolverine is presently the member of:
   A) The X-Men Blue Strike Force
   B) The X-Men Gold Strike Force
   C) X-Factor
   D) none of the above—he now fights alone

4) Storm has the power to:
   A) change the weather
   B) turn herself into a tornado
   C) make really scary faces
   D) live in a thundercloud

5) The name of the X-Men's headquarters is:
   A) classified
   B) the X-House
   C) the X-Men Mansion
   D) The Pro-Mutant Right to Life, Liberty, and the Pursuit of Happiness Political Action Committee

6) Before he joined X-Force, Shatterstar lived:
   A) at home
   B) in the past
   C) in the future
   D) above a Chinese restaurant

7) Dark Phoenix is:
   A) something your mother gives you to drink when you're really sick
   B) a villain who destroyed a solar system
   C) a really hot sports car that Wolverine drives
   D) none of the above

8) What is Magneto's real name?
   A) Magnus
   B) Mr. Attraction
   C) no one knows
   D) Sir

9) Rogue wears a bodysuit because:
   A) she has a severe case of skin rash
   B) she does commercials for a sportswear company
   C) she wants to protect her friends from her uncontrollable power-stealing ability
   D) all of the above

10) Havok is:
   A) Storm's stepbrother
   B) Cyclops's brother
   C) Professor X's nephew
   D) the guy who always gets into trouble at parties

Answers are on page 80.

Most Valuable X-Men Comics

Lots of people save their comic books. Are those comics worth anything? Most of them are pretty reasonably priced. But some of the comics about the X-Men are worth a lot. Below is a list of some of the most valuable comics starring the X-Men. You'll notice that we included a couple of titles, like *The Incredible Hulk #181*, because they include important X-Men history, such as the first appearance of Wolverine.

Now, keep in mind that the prices listed are only a guide! Depending on where you live and where you shop, and the condition of the comic itself, you may find the price to be either higher or lower.

THE UNCANNY X-MEN #1	**$1,900.00**
THE UNCANNY X-MEN #2	**$420.00**
THE UNCANNY X-MEN #3	**$220.00**
THE UNCANNY X-MEN #4	**$180.00**
THE UNCANNY X-MEN #5	**$145.00**
THE UNCANNY X-MEN #6–10	**$110.00 each**
THE UNCANNY X-MEN #94	**$140.00**
GIANT-SIZE X-MEN #1	**$105.00**
THE INCREDIBLE HULK #181	**$260.00**
WOLVERINE Limited Series #1	**$18.00**
X-FACTOR #1	**$8.00**

TM

Wolverine

X-tra Bonus: A Mutant Checklist

There are far more mutants in the pages of the comics than can possibly be covered in this book. We couldn't leave you without giving you a complete mutant checklist.

The Good Guys

Archangel
Banshee
Beast
Bishop
Boom Boom
Cable
Cannonball
Cerise
Changeling
Colossus
Cyclops
Cypher
Dazzler
Domino
Feral
Firestar
Forge
Gambit

Havok
Iceman
Jubilee
Karma
Kylun
Lockheed
Longshot
Magik
Magma
Marvel Girl
Maverick
Meggan
Mimic
Mirage
Multiple Man
Nightcrawler
Phoenix I
Phoenix II

Polaris
Professor X
Psylocke
Quicksilver
Rogue
Shadowcat
Shatterstar
Siryn
Storm
Strong Guy
Sunfire
Sunspot
Thunderbird
Warlock
Widget
Wolfsbane
Wolverine

TM

Magneto

The Bad Guys

Apocalypse
Black Queen
Black Tom
Blob
Brood
Brotherhood of
   Evil Mutants
Caliban
Dark Phoenix
Deadpool
Deathbird
Gatecrasher
Gideon
Juggernaut

Lady Deathstryke
Magneto
Masque
Mastermind
Mesmero
Mojo
Mojo II
Mr. Sinister
Mutant Liberation
   Front
Mutates
Mystique
Omega Red
Proteus
Pyro

Sabretooth
Saturnyne
Sauron
Sentinels
Shadow King
Shiva
Stryfe
Technet
Toad
Unus
Upstarts
Vanisher
Warwolves
White Queen

Mutant X-pert Answers: 1:C, 2:B, 3:A, 4:A, 5:C, 6:C, 7:B, 8:C, 9:C, 10:B